CYBER SECURE

Safe Guarding our Digital Borders

Geoffrey Zachary

CONTENTS

Cyber secure: Safeguarding Our Digital Borders

PART I: UNDERSTANDING THE CYBERSECURITY LANDSCAPE

CHAPTER 1: THE EVOLVING CYBER THREAT LANDSCAPE

In today's interconnected digital world, the threat landscape of cybersecurity is constantly evolving, posing significant challenges to individuals, organizations, and governments. This chapter provides an overview of the ever-changing cyber threat landscape, exploring the nature of cyber threats, their impact, and the need for robust cybersecurity measures.

The digital age has brought unprecedented opportunities for innovation and collaboration, but it has also opened up new avenues for malicious actors to exploit vulnerabilities in our digital infrastructure. Cyber threats encompass a wide range of malicious activities, including hacking, malware attacks, data breaches, identity theft, and ransomware. These threats can disrupt critical services, compromise sensitive information, and undermine trust in digital systems.

One example of a significant cyber threat is the rise of ransomware attacks. Ransomware is a type of malware that encrypts a victim's data, rendering it inaccessible until a ransom is paid. These attacks have targeted organizations of all sizes, from small businesses to large corporations, and have had devastating consequences. The WannaCry ransomware attack in 2017 affected hundreds of thousands of computers worldwide, disrupting healthcare systems, transportation networks, and businesses.

Another growing concern is the increasing sophistication of nation-state-sponsored cyberattacks. These attacks involve state-sponsored actors targeting critical infrastructure, government agencies, and even election systems. For instance, the NotPetya malware, believed to be linked to a nation-state, caused widespread damage in 2017, affecting organizations globally and resulting in billions of dollars in losses.

The impact of cyber threats extends beyond financial losses. They can erode public trust, compromise personal privacy, and undermine national security. Organizations face reputational damage, legal liabilities, and regulatory penalties in the aftermath of a cyber incident. Individuals can experience significant personal and financial harm as their personal information is compromised.

To combat the evolving cyber threat landscape, it is crucial for individuals and organizations to adopt proactive cybersecurity measures. This includes implementing strong access controls, regularly updating software and systems, conducting regular security assessments, and educating employees on best practices for online security.

Governments also play a critical role in addressing cyber threats. They must establish robust cybersecurity policies, invest in cybersecurity research and development, and promote information sharing and collaboration among public and private entities. International cooperation is essential, as cyber threats transcend national boundaries and require a collective response.

Real-life examples of cyber threats and their impact serve as a stark reminder of the evolving cyber threat landscape. The 2013 Target data breach, where hackers gained access to personal and financial information of millions of customers, highlighted the vulnerabilities in retail systems and the need for improved cybersecurity practices. The Stuxnet worm, discovered in 2010, demonstrated the potential of cyberattacks to target critical infrastructure, as it specifically targeted industrial control systems.

In conclusion, the cyber threat landscape continues to evolve, posing significant challenges to individuals, organizations, and governments. Understanding the nature of cyber threats, their impact, and adopting proactive cybersecurity measures are crucial in safeguarding digital systems and protecting sensitive information. The examples of real-life cyber threats remind us of the importance of maintaining vigilance and investing in robust cybersecurity practices to mitigate the risks posed by an ever-evolving cyber threat landscape.

CHAPTER 2:
THE IMPACT OF CYBERSECURITY BREACHES ON INDIVIDUALS AND ORGANISATIONS

Cybersecurity breaches have become a prevalent and costly issue in today's digital landscape. This chapter delves into the profound impact that cybersecurity breaches can have on individuals and organizations, exploring the far-reaching consequences of these breaches and the importance of robust cybersecurity measures.

Cybersecurity breaches can have devastating effects on individuals. One significant impact is the compromise of personal and sensitive information. When hackers gain unauthorized access to personal data, it can lead to identity theft, financial fraud, and invasion of privacy. For example, the Equifax data breach in 2017 exposed the personal information of over 147 million people, including their social security numbers and credit card details. This breach had severe repercussions for individuals, who faced the risk of identity theft and financial losses.

Organizations also bear the brunt of cybersecurity breaches. The financial impact can be substantial, encompassing direct costs such as incident response, remediation, and regulatory fines, as well as indirect costs such as reputational damage and loss of customer trust. The 2013 data breach at Target, a major U.S. retailer, resulted in a loss of $162 million in expenses related to the breach, including legal settlements and other costs.

Reputational damage is another significant consequence of cybersecurity breaches. When organizations fail to protect sensitive information, it erodes public trust and damages their brand reputation. This can result in a loss of customers and business opportunities. The Yahoo data breach in 2013, where billions of user accounts were compromised, not only led to financial losses but also severely impacted Yahoo's reputation and resulted in a reduced acquisition offer from Verizon.

The impact of cybersecurity breaches extends beyond financial and reputational consequences. Critical infrastructure, such as power grids, transportation systems, and healthcare facilities, is increasingly targeted by cybercriminals. A notable example is the 2015 cyberattack on Ukraine's power grid, which left hundreds of thousands of people without electricity. This incident highlighted the vulnerabilities of critical infrastructure to cyber threats and the potential for widespread disruption.

Small and medium-sized enterprises (SMEs) are also vulnerable to cybersecurity breaches. These businesses often have limited resources and cybersecurity expertise, making them attractive targets for cybercriminals. The impact of breaches on SMEs can be particularly severe, as they may lack the financial resilience and recovery capabilities of larger organizations. The 2019 ransomware attack on the City of Baltimore's computer systems resulted in significant disruptions to city services and incurred costs of over $18 million in recovery and remediation efforts.

Real-life examples of cybersecurity breaches serve as stark reminders of the impact on individuals and organizations. The

2014 breach of the U.S. Office of Personnel Management (OPM) exposed sensitive information of millions of federal employees, including background investigation records and fingerprints. This breach not only compromised national security but also had long-lasting consequences for individuals whose personal information was exposed.

In conclusion, cybersecurity breaches have far-reaching consequences for individuals and organizations. The compromise of personal information, financial losses, reputational damage, and disruptions to critical infrastructure highlight the importance of robust cybersecurity measures. Real-life examples demonstrate the profound impact of breaches on individuals and organizations, underscoring the urgent need for vigilance and investment in cybersecurity practices. Mitigating the risks of cybersecurity breaches requires a proactive and comprehensive approach to safeguarding digital systems and protecting sensitive information.

CHAPTER 3: THE COST OF CYBERATTACKS: ECONOMIC AND REPUTATIONAL CONSEQUENCES

In today's interconnected world, cyberattacks have emerged as a significant threat to businesses and individuals alike. This chapter explores the profound economic and reputational consequences of cyberattacks, shedding light on the high costs associated with these malicious activities.

Economic Consequences:
Cyberattacks impose substantial financial burdens on individuals and organizations. The direct costs include expenses related to incident response, investigation, recovery, and legal proceedings. Additionally, there are indirect costs that often surpass the immediate financial impact. These include reputational damage, loss of customer trust, and long-term business implications.

Real-life examples illustrate the economic consequences of cyberattacks. The 2017 WannaCry ransomware attack infected hundreds of thousands of computers globally, causing an estimated $4 billion in financial damages. Organizations affected by this attack incurred significant costs in terms of system restoration, lost productivity, and reputational damage. Similarly, the NotPetya malware attack in 2017 resulted in losses of around $10 billion for affected businesses, including global shipping giant Maersk, which reported losses of over $300 million.

Reputational Consequences:
One of the most significant and long-lasting impacts of cyberattacks is reputational damage. When customer data is compromised or services are disrupted, it erodes trust and tarnishes the reputation of affected organizations. Rebuilding trust and restoring a damaged reputation can take years and may require substantial investments in marketing and public relations efforts.

A prime example of reputational damage caused by a cyberattack is the 2013 data breach at Target. The attack compromised the personal information of approximately 40 million customers and resulted in a significant loss of trust among consumers. Target's reputation suffered, leading to a decline in sales, customer loyalty, and stock value.

The Equifax data breach in 2017 is another prominent case that illustrates the reputational consequences of cyberattacks. The breach exposed the personal information of 147 million individuals, leading to widespread criticism and a loss of confidence in the company's ability to protect sensitive data. Equifax faced public backlash, legal consequences, and a decline in its stock price.

Beyond the immediate financial and reputational impacts, cyberattacks can have long-term consequences for businesses. Organizations may face regulatory fines and legal liabilities, especially in cases where they fail to comply with data protection regulations. Additionally, the loss of intellectual property and trade secrets can diminish a company's competitive advantage, impacting its future growth and profitability.

Small and medium-sized enterprises (SMEs) are particularly

vulnerable to the economic and reputational consequences of cyberattacks. These businesses often lack the financial resources and cybersecurity expertise to effectively respond to and recover from an attack. The Ponemon Institute's 2020 Cost of Cybercrime study found that the average cost of a data breach for SMEs was $2.45 million.

In conclusion, cyberattacks impose significant economic and reputational consequences on individuals and organizations. The direct and indirect costs can be substantial, affecting financial stability, customer trust, and long-term business prospects. Real-life examples highlight the devastating impact of cyberattacks, emphasizing the need for proactive cybersecurity measures and robust incident response plans. Organizations must invest in cybersecurity to mitigate the risks and protect themselves from the potentially devastating consequences of cyberattacks.

CHAPTER 4: THE ROLE OF GOVERNMENT AND LAW ENFORCEMENT IN CYBERSECURITY

Cybersecurity is a complex and ever-evolving field, and the responsibility of protecting individuals, organizations, and critical infrastructure falls not only on the shoulders of private entities but also on governments and law enforcement agencies. This chapter explores the vital role of government and law enforcement in cybersecurity, focusing on their efforts to combat cyber threats, enforce regulations, and promote a safe and secure digital environment.

1. Developing Cybersecurity Policies and Regulations:
Governments play a crucial role in establishing cybersecurity policies and regulations to protect their citizens and national interests. They formulate frameworks that guide organizations in implementing cybersecurity measures, setting standards for data protection, incident response, and risk management. These policies are designed to ensure the security and resilience of critical infrastructure sectors such as energy, finance, healthcare, and transportation.

Real-life examples demonstrate the role of government in cybersecurity regulation. The European Union's General Data

Protection Regulation (GDPR), implemented in 2018, sets strict rules for the protection of personal data and imposes significant penalties on organizations that fail to comply. The Cybersecurity Law of China, enacted in 2017, establishes guidelines for data protection, network security, and the conduct of critical infrastructure operators.

2. Enhancing Cybercrime Investigation and Prosecution:
Law enforcement agencies play a critical role in investigating and prosecuting cybercriminals. They work closely with cybersecurity experts and intelligence agencies to identify, track, and apprehend individuals and groups engaged in cybercrimes. Their efforts aim to disrupt cybercriminal networks, dismantle botnets, and bring offenders to justice.

Real-life examples showcase the collaboration between law enforcement agencies and cybersecurity experts. Operation Darkode, an international law enforcement operation conducted in 2015, successfully dismantled a notorious hacking forum that facilitated the sale of stolen data, malware, and hacking tools. The operation involved the cooperation of law enforcement agencies from 20 countries, leading to numerous arrests and the takedown of the criminal infrastructure.

3. Strengthening Public-Private Partnerships:
Effective cybersecurity requires collaboration between the public and private sectors. Governments work closely with industry leaders, academia, and cybersecurity professionals to share threat intelligence, best practices, and technological advancements. Public-private partnerships facilitate information sharing, incident response coordination, and the development of joint initiatives to address emerging cyber threats.

Real-life examples highlight successful public-private partnerships. The National Cybersecurity Centre of Excellence (NCCoE) in the United States collaborates with industry partners to develop practical cybersecurity solutions and best practices for various sectors. The UK's Cyber Security Information Sharing Partnership (CiSP) facilitates information sharing among government entities, law enforcement, and businesses to enhance cybersecurity resilience.

4. Promoting International Cooperation:
Cyber threats are not confined by national borders, making international cooperation crucial in combating cybercrime and establishing global cybersecurity norms. Governments engage in diplomatic efforts, bilateral agreements, and international treaties to foster cooperation in areas such as information sharing, capacity building, and the extradition of cybercriminals.

Real-life examples highlight the importance of international cooperation in cybersecurity. The Budapest Convention on Cybercrime, adopted by the Council of Europe, provides a framework for international cooperation in combating cybercrime, harmonizing legislation, and facilitating cross-border investigations. The Five Eyes alliance, comprising intelligence agencies from the United States, the United Kingdom, Canada, Australia, and New Zealand, collaborates on cyber threat intelligence and information sharing.

In conclusion, the role of government and law enforcement in cybersecurity is essential for safeguarding individuals, organizations, and critical infrastructure. Governments establish cybersecurity policies and regulations, law enforcement agencies investigate and prosecute cybercriminals, public-private partnerships enhance collaboration, and international cooperation fosters a united front against cyber threats. Real-life examples demonstrate the tangible impact of government and law enforcement efforts in promoting a safe and secure digital environment. By working together, governments, law enforcement agencies, and the private sector can effectively combat cyber threats and ensure the resilience of our digital world.

PART II: FUNDAMENTALS OF CYBERSECURITY

CHAPTER 5: INTRODUCTION TO CYBERSECURITY: PRINCIPLES AND CONCEPTS

In an increasingly digital world, cybersecurity has become a critical aspect of our daily lives. This chapter provides an introduction to the fundamental principles and concepts of cybersecurity, exploring the key elements necessary to protect individuals, organizations, and systems from cyber threats. By understanding these principles, individuals can take proactive measures to enhance their online security and contribute to a safer digital environment.

1. Confidentiality, Integrity, and Availability (CIA) Triad:
The CIA triad forms the foundation of cybersecurity. Confidentiality ensures that information is accessed only by authorized individuals, integrity ensures the accuracy and trustworthiness of data, and availability ensures that systems and data are accessible when needed. Protecting the CIA triad is crucial in maintaining the security and functionality of digital systems.

Real-life example: Encryption is an essential technique used to maintain confidentiality. The use of secure communication channels, such as Transport Layer Security (TLS), ensures that sensitive information transmitted over the internet remains confidential and protected from unauthorized access.

2. Risk Management:

Risk management involves identifying, assessing, and mitigating potential risks to information systems and data. It encompasses the processes of risk identification, risk analysis, risk evaluation, and risk treatment. By understanding and managing risks effectively, individuals and organizations can make informed decisions to protect their digital assets.

Real-life example: The National Institute of Standards and Technology (NIST) provides a risk management framework that guides organizations in assessing and managing cybersecurity risks. This framework helps organizations identify vulnerabilities, prioritize actions, and allocate resources effectively to protect against cyber threats.

3. Defence in Depth:

Défense in depth is a layered approach to cybersecurity that involves implementing multiple security measures at various levels to provide overlapping protection. This approach ensures that even if one layer is breached, other layers are in place to prevent further unauthorized access or damage.

Real-life example: A defence-in-depth strategy may include measures such as firewalls, intrusion detection systems, antivirus software, access controls, and employee awareness training. These multiple layers of security work together to create a robust defence against cyber threats.

4. Security Awareness and Training:

Human behaviour plays a significant role in cybersecurity. Security awareness and training programs educate individuals about common cyber threats, best practices for secure online behaviour, and the importance of maintaining good cybersecurity hygiene. By raising awareness and providing training, individuals can become an integral part of the cybersecurity defence.

Real-life example: The "Stop. Think. Connect." campaign, led by the National Cyber Security Alliance, promotes safe online practices, and encourages individuals to think critically before sharing sensitive information or clicking on suspicious links. Such campaigns aim to empower individuals to protect themselves and their digital assets.

5. Emerging Threats and Technologies:
Cybersecurity is a constantly evolving field, with new threats and technologies emerging regularly. Staying updated with the latest cybersecurity trends and understanding emerging technologies, such as artificial intelligence, Internet of Things (IoT), and cloud computing, is crucial to effectively address the evolving cyber landscape.

Real-life example: The rise of ransomware attacks, where malicious actors encrypt a victim's data and demand a ransom for its release, has become a significant cybersecurity threat. Organizations must implement robust backup systems and educate employees about the risks to mitigate the impact of such attacks.

In conclusion, understanding the fundamental principles and concepts of cybersecurity is essential for individuals and organizations to protect themselves from cyber threats. The CIA triad, risk management, defence in depth, security awareness and training, and staying updated with emerging threats and technologies are crucial elements of a comprehensive cybersecurity approach. Real-life examples demonstrate the practical application of these principles and concepts, emphasizing the importance of proactive cybersecurity measures in today's digital landscape. By implementing these principles, individuals can enhance their online security and contribute to a safer and more secure digital world.

CHAPTER 6:
NETWORK SECURITY:
PROTECTING
THE DIGITAL
INFRASTRUCTURE

Network security is a crucial component of cybersecurity, as it focuses on protecting the digital infrastructure and data that traverse computer networks. This chapter explores the principles, technologies, and best practices involved in safeguarding network environments from cyber threats. By understanding network security, individuals and organizations can implement effective measures to ensure the confidentiality, integrity, and availability of their network resources.

1. Network Segmentation:
Network segmentation involves dividing a network into smaller, isolated segments to limit the potential impact of a security breach. By implementing separate network segments, organizations can control access privileges, contain threats, and minimize lateral movement within the network.

Real-life example: In the banking industry, network segmentation is commonly used to separate sensitive financial data from other areas of the network. This approach helps protect customer information and financial transactions, reducing the risk of unauthorized access or compromise.

2. Firewalls:

Firewalls act as a barrier between internal networks and external networks, monitoring and controlling incoming and outgoing network traffic based on predefined security rules. They help prevent unauthorized access and filter out potentially malicious traffic.

Real-life example: A next-generation firewall can analyse network traffic at the application layer, enabling granular control over specific applications and detecting sophisticated threats such as advanced malware or command-and-control communications.

3. Intrusion Detection and Prevention Systems (IDPS):

IDPSs monitor network traffic in real-time, identifying and responding to potential security threats or policy violations. They can detect and prevent unauthorized access attempts, malicious activities, and network anomalies.

Real-life example: An IDPS can detect and alert administrators about suspicious network activities, such as multiple failed logins attempts or a sudden surge in network traffic from a specific source. This helps mitigate the risk of a cyber-attack before it causes significant damage.

4. Virtual Private Networks (VPNs):

VPNs provide secure remote access to internal networks over the internet by encrypting data transmissions. They establish an encrypted tunnel between the user's device and the network, ensuring the confidentiality and integrity of data in transit.

Real-life example: Many organizations use VPNs to enable their remote workforce to securely access corporate resources from any location. This is particularly important when employees connect to public Wi-Fi networks, which can be vulnerable to eavesdropping and data interception.

5. Wireless Network Security:

Securing wireless networks is crucial to prevent unauthorized access and protect sensitive information. This involves implementing strong encryption protocols, enforcing access controls, and regularly updating wireless network equipment.

Real-life example: The Wi-Fi Protected Access 3 (WPA3) protocol is the latest standard for securing wireless networks. It provides enhanced encryption, protects against offline password-guessing attacks, and ensures stronger security for devices connecting to Wi-Fi networks.

6. Threat Intelligence and Monitoring:

Threat intelligence involves collecting, analysing, and sharing information about known and emerging cyber threats. Network monitoring tools help detect and respond to potential security incidents in real-time, enabling proactive threat mitigation.

Real-life example: Security Operations Centres (SOCs) use threat intelligence feeds and advanced monitoring tools to detect and respond to security incidents. By continuously monitoring network traffic and analysing threat intelligence data, SOC teams can identify and mitigate potential threats promptly.

In conclusion, network security plays a vital role in protecting the digital infrastructure and data within computer networks. Implementing network segmentation, firewalls, IDPSs, VPNs, wireless network security measures, and robust threat intelligence and monitoring practices are essential for safeguarding network environments. Real-life examples demonstrate the practical application of these network security measures, highlighting their significance in preventing unauthorized access, detecting potential threats, and ensuring the integrity and availability of network resources. By understanding and implementing these network security principles and technologies, individuals and organizations can fortify their networks against cyber threats and maintain a secure digital infrastructure.

CHAPTER 7: DATA PROTECTION AND ENCRYPTION

Data protection and encryption are essential aspects of cybersecurity that focus on safeguarding sensitive information from unauthorized access and ensuring its confidentiality, integrity, and availability. This chapter explores the principles, techniques, and best practices involved in data protection and encryption. By implementing robust data protection measures, individuals and organizations can mitigate the risk of data breaches and maintain the privacy and security of their valuable data assets.

1. Importance of Data Protection:
Data protection is critical as it ensures the security and privacy of sensitive information, such as personal data, financial records, and intellectual property. By implementing data protection measures, organizations can maintain customer trust, comply with regulatory requirements, and prevent the potential consequences of data breaches.

Real-life example: The European Union's General Data Protection Regulation (GDPR) sets strict guidelines for data protection and privacy. Organizations that fail to comply with GDPR can face significant financial penalties and reputational damage.

2. Encryption:

Encryption is a cryptographic technique that transforms data into an unreadable format using algorithms and cryptographic keys. Encrypted data can only be decrypted and accessed with the corresponding decryption key, providing an additional layer of protection against unauthorized access.

Real-life example: Transport Layer Security (TLS) and Secure Sockets Layer (SSL) protocols are widely used to encrypt data transmitted over the internet, ensuring secure communication between web browsers and servers. This protects sensitive information, such as credit card details and login credentials, from interception and unauthorized disclosure.

3. Symmetric Encryption:
Symmetric encryption uses a single shared key to both encrypt and decrypt data. This key must be securely exchanged between the sender and the intended recipient. Symmetric encryption is fast and efficient but requires secure key management.

Real-life example: The Advanced Encryption Standard (AES) is a widely used symmetric encryption algorithm that provides strong security and performance. It is employed in various applications, including secure messaging, disk encryption, and wireless network security.

4. Asymmetric Encryption:
Asymmetric encryption, also known as public-key encryption, uses a pair of mathematically related keys: a public key for encryption and a private key for decryption. The public key can be freely distributed, while the private key must be kept confidential.

Real-life example: The Pretty Good Privacy (PGP) encryption software utilizes asymmetric encryption to secure email communications. The sender encrypts the email using the recipient's public key, ensuring that only the intended recipient, holding the corresponding private key, can decrypt and read the message.

5. Hash Functions:

Hash functions convert data of arbitrary size into a fixed-size hash value. Hashing is commonly used to verify the integrity of data and detect any changes or tampering. Even a slight modification in the data will result in a significantly different hash value.

Real-life example: The Secure Hash Algorithm (SHA) family, including SHA-256 and SHA-3, is widely used in digital signatures, password storage, and data integrity checks. These algorithms generate hash values that are extremely difficult to reverse-engineer, providing assurance of data integrity.

6. Data Loss Prevention (DLP):

Data Loss Prevention aims to prevent the accidental or intentional disclosure of sensitive data. DLP solutions employ various techniques, such as content inspection, encryption, and user activity monitoring, to detect and prevent data leakage.

Real-life example: A financial institution might implement DLP software to prevent employees from transmitting sensitive customer information via unsecured channels, such as personal email accounts or USB drives, thus reducing the risk of data breaches and regulatory non-compliance.

In conclusion, data protection and encryption are vital components of cybersecurity that ensure the security, privacy, and integrity of sensitive information. Implementing encryption techniques, such as symmetric and asymmetric encryption, along with hash functions and data loss prevention measures, helps mitigate the risk of data breaches and unauthorized access. Real-life examples demonstrate the practical applications of these data protection measures, highlighting their significance in securing sensitive data, complying with regulations, and maintaining customer trust. By understanding and implementing robust data protection and encryption practices, individuals and organizations can safeguard their valuable data assets and reduce the potential impact of data breaches.

CHAPTER 8:
SECURE CODING
AND APPLICATION
DEVELOPMENT

Secure coding and application development are crucial components of cybersecurity that focus on building resilient and secure software systems. This chapter explores the principles, best practices, and techniques involved in secure coding and application development. By incorporating security measures throughout the software development lifecycle, developers can mitigate the risk of vulnerabilities and ensure the integrity and confidentiality of their applications.

1. Importance of Secure Coding:
Secure coding is essential as it helps prevent common vulnerabilities, such as injection attacks, cross-site scripting (XSS), and insecure direct object references. By following secure coding practices, developers can build applications that are more resistant to malicious exploitation and protect user data.

Real-life example: The Heartbleed vulnerability, which affected the OpenSSL cryptographic library, exposed millions of websites, and their users to potential data breaches. This incident highlighted the critical importance of secure coding practices to prevent vulnerabilities that can be exploited by attackers.

2. Input Validation and Sanitization:

Input validation and sanitization are crucial for preventing code injection attacks. Developers should validate and sanitize all user input to ensure it meets the expected format and prevent unauthorized execution of malicious code.

Real-life example: The SQL Injection attack is a common vulnerability where attackers can inject malicious SQL statements through user input fields, potentially accessing or manipulating sensitive database information. Implementing input validation and sanitization can mitigate the risk of such attacks.

3. Secure Authentication and Authorization:

Proper authentication and authorization mechanisms are essential for ensuring that only authorized users can access sensitive functionality and data. Developers should implement strong authentication methods and enforce appropriate authorization controls based on user roles and permissions.

Real-life example: The breach of the Equifax credit reporting agency in 2017 was a result of inadequate authentication and authorization practices, allowing attackers to gain unauthorized access to sensitive customer data. Secure authentication and authorization practices could have prevented or mitigated the impact of this breach.

4. Secure Session Management:

Effective session management is crucial for maintaining the security and privacy of user sessions. Developers should implement measures such as session timeouts, secure session handling, and protection against session hijacking or fixation attacks.

Real-life example: The vulnerability known as Session Fixation can allow attackers to manipulate session identifiers and gain unauthorized access to user accounts. Secure session management practices, such as generating unique session identifiers and invalidating old sessions upon authentication, can mitigate the risk of this vulnerability.

5. Error Handling and Logging:
Proper error handling and logging practices help identify and mitigate security issues, as well as aid in troubleshooting and incident response. Developers should implement secure error handling mechanisms that do not disclose sensitive information and log relevant security events for analysis.

Real-life example: The lack of proper error handling and logging in the infamous 2013 Target data breach allowed attackers to infiltrate the network, steal customer data, and evade detection for an extended period. Robust error handling and logging practices can provide valuable insights into security incidents and aid in timely response.

6. Secure Code Review and Testing:
Regular code reviews and comprehensive security testing, including static and dynamic analysis, are crucial for identifying vulnerabilities and ensuring the overall security of the application. Developers should perform thorough security assessments to detect and remediate potential weaknesses in the codebase.

Real-life example: The Open Web Application Security Project (OWASP) Top 10 list highlights common web application vulnerabilities, such as cross-site scripting (XSS) and cross-site request forgery (CSRF). Conducting secure code reviews and testing helps identify and address these vulnerabilities to prevent potential attacks.

In conclusion, secure coding and application development are essential practices for building robust and secure software systems. By incorporating input validation and sanitization, secure authentication and authorization, secure session management, error handling and logging, and regular code reviews and testing, developers can mitigate the risk of vulnerabilities and protect user data. Real-life examples highlight the significance of secure coding practices in preventing data breaches and unauthorized access to sensitive information. By following secure coding principles, developers can contribute to a more secure digital landscape and protect users' privacy and trust in applications.

CHAPTER 9: USER AUTHENTICATION AND ACCESS CONTROL

User authentication and access control are essential aspects of cybersecurity that aim to ensure that only authorized individuals can access resources and perform specific actions within a system. This chapter explores the principles, techniques, and best practices associated with user authentication and access control, highlighting their significance in safeguarding sensitive information and mitigating the risk of unauthorized access.

1. Importance of User Authentication:
User authentication is the process of verifying the identity of an individual requesting access to a system or application. It is crucial for establishing trust and ensuring that only authorized users can gain entry.

Real-life example: Two-factor authentication (2FA) is a widely adopted method that adds an additional layer of security to user authentication. It requires users to provide a second form of verification, such as a unique code sent to their mobile device, in addition to their password. This helps protect against unauthorized access, even if the password is compromised.

2. Authentication Factors:
Authentication typically involves the use of multiple factors to establish a user's identity. These factors can be categorized into

three types: knowledge factors (e.g., passwords, PINs), possession factors (e.g., physical tokens, mobile devices), and inherent factors (e.g., biometrics like fingerprints or facial recognition).

Real-life example: Many mobile devices now offer biometric authentication, such as fingerprint or facial recognition, to unlock the device or access certain applications. These technologies provide a convenient and secure means of authentication, as they rely on unique biometric traits that are difficult to replicate.

3. Access Control Policies:
Access control is the practice of granting or restricting access to resources based on predefined policies. Access control policies define who can access specific resources, what actions they can perform, and under what conditions access is granted or denied.

Real-life example: Role-based access control (RBAC) is a commonly used access control model that assigns roles to users and defines the permissions associated with each role. For example, within a company's network, an employee may have the role of "manager" with access to sensitive information, while a regular employee may have a "user" role with limited access.

4. Multi-factor Authentication (MFA):
Multi-factor authentication (MFA) enhances the security of user authentication by requiring the use of multiple independent authentication factors. It combines different types of authentication factors, such as passwords, physical tokens, or biometrics, to strengthen the authentication process.

Real-life example: Online banking platforms often employ MFA to protect user accounts. In addition to the username and password, users may be required to enter a one-time password (OTP) sent to their registered mobile number or use a physical security token. This multi-layered authentication approach significantly reduces the risk of unauthorized access.

5. Single Sign-On (SSO):

Single sign-on (SSO) is a mechanism that allows users to authenticate once and gain access to multiple applications or systems without needing to re-enter their credentials. It simplifies the login process for users while maintaining security.

Real-life example: Many organizations adopt SSO solutions to streamline access to various internal applications. For instance, employees can log in to a central portal using their credentials and seamlessly access other tools and systems without the need for separate authentication.

6. Privileged Access Management (PAM):
Privileged access management (PAM) focuses on managing and securing privileged accounts, which have elevated privileges and access rights within a system. PAM solutions help control and monitor privileged access to prevent misuse or unauthorized activities.

Real-life example: The 2017 breach of Equifax was a result of unauthorized access to sensitive data through a privileged account. Implementing robust PAM practices, including strong access controls and regular monitoring, can help mitigate the risk of such incidents.

In conclusion, user authentication and access control are crucial components of cybersecurity that ensure only authorized individuals can access resources and perform specific actions. Real-life examples, such as multi-factor authentication, role-based access control, and privileged access management, highlight the significance of these practices in protecting sensitive information and preventing unauthorized access. By implementing strong authentication mechanisms, defining granular access control policies, and utilizing technologies like multi-factor authentication and single sign-on, organizations can enhance their security posture and safeguard against potential threats.

PART III:
CYBERSECURITY
BEST PRACTICES

CHAPTER 10: BUILDING A SECURE DIGITAL ENVIRONMENT: POLICIES AND PROCEDURES

Creating a secure digital environment is paramount in protecting sensitive information and mitigating cybersecurity risks. This chapter explores the importance of establishing robust policies and procedures that govern the use of technology and guide employees in adhering to best practices. It delves into the key elements of a comprehensive security framework and provides real-life examples to illustrate their effectiveness in safeguarding organizations' digital assets.

1. The Role of Policies and Procedures:
Policies and procedures form the foundation of a secure digital environment. They provide guidelines and instructions for employees, outlining acceptable behaviour, security protocols, and responsibilities regarding the use of technology.

Real-life example: An acceptable use policy (AUP) is a common policy implemented by organizations to define acceptable and unacceptable use of company resources, including computer systems, networks, and software. It sets clear expectations for employees and helps protect against unauthorized or inappropriate use of technology.

2. Information Security Policies:
Information security policies define the framework for protecting an organization's information assets. They address areas such as data classification, data handling, access control, incident response, and encryption.

Real-life example: The Payment Card Industry Data Security Standard (PCI DSS) is a set of security standards designed to protect cardholder data during payment card transactions. Organizations that process, store, or transmit cardholder data must comply with these policies to maintain the security and integrity of customer payment information.

3. Security Awareness and Training:
Security awareness and training programs are essential to educate employees about potential threats, security best practices, and their role in maintaining a secure digital environment. Regular training sessions and simulated phishing exercises help raise awareness and reduce the likelihood of human error leading to security incidents.

Real-life example: The "Stop. Think. Connect." campaign, launched by the U.S. Department of Homeland Security, promotes safe online behaviour, and provides resources and tips to individuals and organizations. This campaign aims to increase awareness of cybersecurity risks and empower users to make informed decisions when using technology.

4. Incident Response and Business Continuity Planning:
Incident response and business continuity plans outline the procedures and actions to be taken in the event of a cybersecurity incident or other disruptions. These plans ensure a timely response, minimize the impact of an incident, and facilitate the

recovery and continuity of operations.

Real-life example: The ransomware attack on Colonial Pipeline in 2021 highlighted the importance of incident response and business continuity planning. Promptly activating their incident response plan helped mitigate the impact on operations and expedite the recovery process.

5. Regulatory Compliance:
Organizations must adhere to industry-specific regulations and standards related to data privacy and security. Compliance with regulations such as the General Data Protection Regulation (GDPR) or the Health Insurance Portability and Accountability Act (HIPAA) is critical to protect sensitive information and maintain customer trust.

Real-life example: In 2019, British Airways was fined £20 million ($26 million) by the UK's Information Commissioner's Office for a data breach that compromised the personal and financial information of over 400,000 customers. The incident highlighted the consequences of failing to comply with data protection regulations and the importance of implementing robust security policies and procedures.

In conclusion, building a secure digital environment requires the establishment of comprehensive policies and procedures. Real-life examples, such as acceptable use policies, the PCI DSS, and incident response plans, demonstrate the effectiveness of these measures in protecting organizations' digital assets. By implementing information security policies, conducting regular security awareness training, preparing incident response and business continuity plans, and ensuring regulatory compliance, organizations can establish a strong security posture and safeguard against potential threats.

CHAPTER 11: SECURITY AWARENESS AND TRAINING FOR EMPLOYEES

Ensuring the security of an organization's digital environment heavily relies on the knowledge and actions of its employees. This chapter explores the importance of security awareness and training programs in equipping employees with the necessary skills and knowledge to identify and mitigate cybersecurity risks. It delves into the key components of effective security awareness programs, provides real-life examples of their impact, and discusses strategies for promoting a culture of security within organizations.

1. The Need for Security Awareness and Training:
Employees are often the first line of defence against cyber threats. Security awareness and training programs play a crucial role in educating employees about potential risks, teaching them best practices, and cultivating a security-conscious mindset. These programs aim to empower employees to make informed decisions and take proactive measures to protect sensitive information.

Real-life example: The Human Firewall concept is widely used to emphasize the role of employees in maintaining cybersecurity. By creating a well-informed and vigilant workforce, organizations can strengthen their overall security posture and reduce the likelihood of successful cyber-attacks.

2. Identifying Key Security Risks:
Security awareness programs should focus on educating employees about the various cybersecurity risks they may encounter, such as phishing attacks, social engineering, malware, and data breaches. Employees need to understand the techniques employed by cybercriminals and the potential consequences of a security incident.

Real-life example: The "KnowBe4" platform provides interactive security awareness training and simulated phishing campaigns to organizations. By simulating real-world attack scenarios, employees can develop their ability to identify and respond to potential threats effectively.

3. Best Practices and Security Policies:
Security awareness programs should educate employees about best practices for maintaining a secure digital environment. This includes topics such as strong password management, secure remote working, safe browsing habits, and proper data handling procedures. Employees should also be familiar with the organization's security policies and understand their roles and responsibilities in upholding these policies.

Real-life example: Many organizations implement regular security awareness training sessions that cover topics such as password hygiene, avoiding suspicious links or attachments in emails, and reporting security incidents promptly. These sessions reinforce the organization's security policies and provide practical guidance for employees.

4. Phishing Awareness and Response:
Phishing attacks remain one of the most prevalent and effective methods used by cybercriminals. Security awareness programs should educate employees on how to recognize phishing emails, social engineering techniques, and methods to verify

the authenticity of requests for sensitive information. Training should also cover reporting procedures for suspected phishing attempts.

Real-life example: The "Cofense" platform offers phishing simulation and training programs to organizations. By sending mock phishing emails to employees and tracking their responses, organizations can assess the effectiveness of their training programs and provide targeted remedial training to individuals who may be more susceptible to phishing attacks.

5. Continuous Learning and Engagement:
Cyber threats evolve rapidly, requiring employees to continuously update their knowledge and skills. Security awareness programs should be an ongoing process that includes regular refreshers, newsletters, quizzes, and other engagement activities to reinforce learning and keep cybersecurity top-of-mind for employees.

Real-life example: The National Cyber Security Centre (NCSC) in the UK offers a variety of free resources, including interactive e-learning courses, videos, and newsletters, to help organizations and individuals improve their cyber awareness and understanding.

In conclusion, security awareness and training programs are crucial in empowering employees to become active participants in maintaining a secure digital environment. Real-life examples, such as the Human Firewall concept and platforms like KnowBe4 and Cofense, demonstrate the effectiveness of these programs in raising awareness and reducing the risk of cyber-attacks. By identifying key security risks, promoting best practices, addressing phishing awareness, and fostering continuous learning, organizations can create a culture of security where employees play an active role in safeguarding sensitive information.

CHAPTER 12:
INCIDENT RESPONSE
AND DISASTER
RECOVERY

In today's interconnected and technology-driven world, organizations face an ever-growing threat landscape. Cybersecurity incidents, ranging from data breaches to network outages, can have significant financial, operational, and reputational consequences. This chapter explores the importance of incident response and disaster recovery strategies in mitigating the impact of cybersecurity incidents. It delves into the key components of effective incident response and disaster recovery plans, provides real-life examples of their application, and discusses the critical role they play in maintaining business continuity.

1. Understanding Incident Response and Disaster Recovery:
Incident response is a structured approach to address and manage the aftermath of a cybersecurity incident. It involves identifying, containing, mitigating, and recovering from security breaches, with the ultimate goal of restoring normal operations as quickly as possible. Disaster recovery, on the other hand, focuses on the steps taken to restore critical systems and data after a major disruption or disaster.

Real-life example: The NotPetya ransomware attack in 2017 affected numerous organizations worldwide, including Maersk, a global shipping company. Maersk's incident response and disaster recovery efforts allowed them to recover and resume operations, minimizing the financial impact and demonstrating the importance of preparedness.

2. Incident Response Process:
An effective incident response plan outlines the roles, responsibilities, and steps to be taken in the event of a cybersecurity incident. It includes key activities such as incident identification, containment, eradication, and recovery. The plan should be regularly tested and updated to address emerging threats and changes in the organization's environment.

Real-life example: The National Institute of Standards and Technology (NIST) provides guidelines, such as the Computer Security Incident Handling Guide, that organizations can follow to develop their incident response processes. These guidelines help organizations establish a systematic and effective approach to incident response.

3. Collaboration and Communication:
Successful incident response relies on collaboration and communication among various stakeholders, including IT teams, management, legal counsel, and public relations. Timely and effective communication is essential to coordinate efforts, share information, and mitigate the impact of the incident on the organization's reputation.

Real-life example: The Equifax data breach in 2017 highlighted the importance of communication during a cybersecurity incident. Equifax faced criticism for its delayed public disclosure of the breach, which resulted in significant reputational damage. This example emphasizes the need for transparency and proactive communication during incident response.

4. Disaster Recovery Planning:

Disaster recovery planning involves developing strategies and procedures to restore critical systems, data, and infrastructure following a major disruption. This includes implementing backups, redundancy measures, and alternative infrastructure to minimize downtime and ensure business continuity.

Real-life example: The fire at the OVHcloud data centre in Strasbourg, France, in 2021 resulted in a major outage affecting thousands of websites. Organizations with effective disaster recovery plans in place were able to recover their services more quickly by leveraging backups and redundant infrastructure.

5. Learning from Incidents:

Effective incident response and disaster recovery involve continuous learning and improvement. Organizations should conduct post-incident reviews, known as "lessons learned" sessions, to identify gaps, refine processes, and enhance their overall cybersecurity posture.

Real-life example: The Target data breach in 2013 led to a comprehensive review of the company's incident response and security practices. Target made significant investments in cybersecurity, including the establishment of a dedicated cybersecurity team, to strengthen its incident response capabilities and prevent future incidents.

In conclusion, incident response and disaster recovery are vital components of an organization's cybersecurity strategy. Real-life examples, such as the NotPetya attack and the Equifax data breach, underscore the importance of being prepared and having robust incident response plans in place. By following established processes, fostering collaboration, implementing effective communication strategies, and conducting thorough post-incident reviews, organizations can minimize the impact of cybersecurity incidents and maintain business continuity in the face of evolving threats.

CHAPTER 13: VENDOR MANAGEMENT AND SUPPLY CHAIN SECURITY

In today's interconnected business landscape, organizations rely on a complex network of vendors and suppliers to deliver products and services. While these relationships bring numerous benefits, they also introduce potential risks to an organization's cybersecurity. This chapter explores the importance of vendor management and supply chain security in mitigating cyber threats. It examines the key considerations, best practices, and real-life examples to illustrate the significance of robust vendor management strategies.

1. Understanding Vendor Management:
Vendor management refers to the process of overseeing and controlling the relationships with third-party vendors and suppliers. It involves assessing their capabilities, managing contracts, and ensuring compliance with security standards. A comprehensive vendor management program helps organizations reduce vulnerabilities and strengthen their overall cybersecurity posture.

Real-life example: The SolarWinds supply chain attack in 2020 demonstrated the criticality of effective vendor management. The attackers infiltrated the software supply chain, compromising SolarWinds' update mechanism and subsequently infecting numerous organizations. This incident highlighted the need for robust security measures and thorough vendor vetting to prevent such attacks.

2. Assessing Vendor Security:
Organizations should conduct thorough assessments of their vendors' security practices and capabilities. This includes evaluating their cybersecurity policies, procedures, and controls, as well as assessing their track record in handling and protecting sensitive data. Assessments can be conducted through questionnaires, on-site audits, or third-party certifications.

Real-life example: In 2019, Capital One experienced a data breach resulting from a vulnerability in a vendor's cloud infrastructure. The incident underscored the importance of assessing the security practices of vendors who have access to an organization's sensitive data and systems.

3. Establishing Security Requirements:
Organizations should clearly define their security requirements and expectations for vendors. This includes specifying minimum security standards, data protection protocols, incident response procedures, and contractual obligations. Vendor contracts should include provisions for regular security assessments, compliance with applicable regulations, and prompt reporting of any security incidents.

Real-life example: The Payment Card Industry Data Security Standard (PCI DSS) includes specific requirements for organizations that handle payment card information. These requirements extend to their vendors, ensuring that security measures are in place throughout the payment card ecosystem.

4. Monitoring and Auditing:
Effective vendor management requires ongoing monitoring and auditing of vendor activities. Regular reviews of security

controls, access privileges, and incident response capabilities help identify and address any potential vulnerabilities or weaknesses. Organizations should also consider conducting periodic penetration tests or vulnerability assessments to assess the resilience of their vendor's systems.

Real-life example: The Target data breach in 2013, which resulted from a compromise of a vendor's credentials, highlighted the importance of continuous monitoring and auditing of vendor activities. Target implemented stronger controls and increased oversight of vendor access to prevent similar incidents in the future.

5. Incident Response and Business Continuity:
Organizations should establish clear incident response and business continuity protocols in collaboration with their vendors. This includes defining roles and responsibilities, conducting joint incident response drills, and developing contingency plans to ensure seamless collaboration during a cybersecurity incident. Regular communication and coordination are essential to minimize the impact of an incident on both parties.

Real-life example: The WannaCry ransomware attack in 2017 disrupted numerous organizations worldwide, including those with critical dependencies on affected vendors. Collaborative incident response efforts were crucial in containing the attack and restoring operations swiftly.

In conclusion, effective vendor management and supply chain security are vital components of a robust cybersecurity strategy. Real-life examples, such as the SolarWinds supply chain attack and the Target data breach, underscore the significance of assessing vendors' security practices, establishing clear requirements, and ongoing monitoring. By implementing comprehensive vendor management programs, organizations can reduce their exposure to cyber risks and maintain the integrity of their supply chain ecosystem.

CHAPTER 14:
CLOUD SECURITY:
SAFEGUARDING DATA
IN THE CLOUD

The widespread adoption of cloud computing has revolutionized the way organizations store, process, and access data. However, the shift to the cloud also introduces new security challenges and risks. This chapter explores the importance of cloud security and provides insights into best practices for safeguarding data in the cloud. Real-life examples will be used to illustrate the significance of robust cloud security measures.

1. Understanding Cloud Security:
Cloud security refers to the set of policies, technologies, and controls implemented to protect data, applications, and infrastructure in cloud environments. It encompasses various aspects, including data privacy, access control, encryption, vulnerability management, and incident response. A comprehensive approach to cloud security is essential to ensure the confidentiality, integrity, and availability of data stored in the cloud.

Real-life example: The 2014 iCloud celebrity photo leak highlighted the importance of cloud security. Attackers exploited weak passwords and security vulnerabilities to gain unauthorized access to celebrities' private photos stored in Apple's iCloud service. This incident emphasized the need for robust authentication mechanisms and encryption to protect sensitive data in the cloud.

2. Assessing Cloud Service Providers:
When selecting a cloud service provider (CSP), organizations should conduct thorough assessments of their security capabilities. This includes evaluating their data protection practices, compliance with industry standards and regulations, incident response procedures, and physical security measures. Organizations should also review the provider's certifications and undergo audits to ensure adherence to security best practices.

Real-life example: In 2017, a misconfigured Amazon Web Services (AWS) S3 bucket exposed sensitive customer data of major organizations, including Verizon, Dow Jones, and the U.S. military. This incident demonstrated the importance of verifying the security configurations and access controls of cloud service providers to prevent accidental exposure of data.

3. Data Encryption and Privacy:
Encrypting data in transit and at rest is crucial for maintaining data confidentiality in the cloud. Organizations should implement strong encryption algorithms and ensure that encryption keys are securely managed. Additionally, they should carefully consider data residency and privacy regulations to ensure compliance when storing sensitive information in the cloud.

Real-life example: The European Union's General Data Protection Regulation (GDPR) imposes strict requirements on the handling and protection of personal data. Organizations storing personal data in the cloud must comply with GDPR's data protection principles and implement appropriate encryption and security measures.

4. Access Control and Identity Management:

Implementing robust access control mechanisms is essential to prevent unauthorized access to cloud resources. Organizations should employ multi-factor authentication, role-based access control, and enforce strong password policies. Additionally, effective identity and access management (IAM) solutions help streamline user provisioning, manage permissions, and monitor user activity in the cloud environment.

Real-life example: The Capital One data breach in 2019 resulted from a misconfigured IAM role that allowed an attacker to access sensitive data stored in the cloud. This incident highlighted the importance of proper access control and regular audits to prevent unauthorized access and privilege escalation.

5. Incident Response and Continuous Monitoring:
Organizations should have incident response plans tailored to cloud environments to effectively detect, respond to, and recover from security incidents. Continuous monitoring and logging of cloud activities enable timely detection of potential threats and anomalies. Regular security assessments, penetration testing, and vulnerability scanning help identify and address security gaps in the cloud environment.

Real-life example: The 2020 Microsoft Exchange Server vulnerabilities demonstrated the need for proactive monitoring and prompt incident response in cloud-based infrastructure. Organizations that detected and addressed the vulnerabilities swiftly mitigated the risk of data breaches and system compromises.

In conclusion, cloud security is paramount for organizations leveraging cloud services to protect their data and ensure operational resilience. Real-life examples, such as the iCloud celebrity photo leak and the Capital One data breach, underscore the importance of assessing cloud service providers, encrypting data, implementing robust access controls, and having effective incident response plans. By following best practices and staying abreast of evolving cloud security threats, organizations can harness the benefits of the cloud while mitigating risks and safeguarding their valuable data.

PART IV: EMERGING TRENDS AND TECHNOLOGIES IN CYBERSECURITY

CHAPTER 15: ARTIFICIAL INTELLIGENCE AND MACHINE LEARNING IN CYBERSECURITY

Artificial Intelligence (AI) and Machine Learning (ML) technologies have emerged as powerful tools in the field of cybersecurity. This chapter explores the role of AI and ML in detecting and mitigating cyber threats, discusses their benefits and challenges, and provides real-life examples of their application in cybersecurity.

1. AI and ML in Cybersecurity:
AI refers to the development of computer systems capable of performing tasks that typically require human intelligence, such as learning, reasoning, and problem-solving. ML is a subset of AI that focuses on the ability of machines to learn and improve from data without explicit programming. In cybersecurity, AI and ML are used to analyse vast amounts of data, identify patterns, detect anomalies, and automate security processes.

2. Benefits of AI and ML in Cybersecurity:
- Enhanced Threat Detection: AI and ML algorithms can analyse large volumes of data in real-time, enabling the detection of sophisticated and evolving cyber threats that may go unnoticed

by traditional security systems.

- Rapid Response and Automation: AI and ML technologies enable the automation of security processes, allowing for faster threat response and mitigation.
- Improved Accuracy: ML algorithms can learn from historical data and refine their models, leading to improved accuracy in identifying and classifying threats.
- Scalability: AI and ML systems can scale to handle the ever-increasing volume of security data, making them well-suited for the dynamic and complex cybersecurity landscape.

3. Challenges of AI and ML in Cybersecurity:
- Adversarial Attacks: Adversaries can exploit vulnerabilities in ML algorithms to manipulate or deceive the system, leading to false negatives or positives.
- Data Quality and Bias: ML models heavily rely on the quality and representativeness of the training data. Biased or incomplete data can result in inaccurate or biased predictions.
- Explainability and Interpretability: The inherent complexity of some AI and ML models makes it challenging to interpret and explain their decision-making process, limiting their adoption in certain regulated industries.

4. Real-Life Examples of AI and ML in Cybersecurity:
- Email Filtering: AI-based email filtering systems use ML algorithms to analyse incoming emails and detect spam, phishing, and malware-laden messages.
- Intrusion Detection: ML models can analyse network traffic patterns and detect anomalous behaviour indicative of a cyberattack, such as unauthorized access or data exfiltration.
- User and Entity Behaviour Analytics (UEBA): AI and ML techniques can analyse user behaviour patterns to identify anomalies and potential insider threats.
- Malware Detection: ML models can analyse file characteristics and behaviour to identify previously unseen malware and malicious code.

- Network Traffic Analysis: ML algorithms can analyse network traffic logs to detect patterns indicative of botnets, DDoS attacks, or other malicious activities.

5. Ethical Considerations and Future Implications:
The use of AI and ML in cybersecurity raises ethical concerns, such as privacy implications and potential biases in decision-making. It is crucial to ensure transparency, accountability, and fairness in the implementation of AI and ML systems. Additionally, ongoing research and development are necessary to address the evolving threat landscape and keep pace with adversaries' tactics.

In conclusion, AI and ML technologies have revolutionized the field of cybersecurity, enabling organizations to detect and respond to cyber threats more effectively. Real-life examples, such as email filtering, intrusion detection, and malware detection, demonstrate the practical application of AI and ML in enhancing security measures. While challenges and ethical considerations exist, the continued advancement and responsible deployment of AI and ML hold great potential for strengthening cyber defences and safeguarding critical systems and data in an increasingly interconnected world.

CHAPTER 16: INTERNET OF THINGS (IOT) SECURITY

The Internet of Things (IoT) has transformed the way we interact with technology, enabling connectivity and automation in various aspects of our lives. However, the proliferation of IoT devices has also raised significant concerns about security and privacy. This chapter explores the importance of IoT security, the risks and vulnerabilities associated with IoT devices, and provides real-life examples to illustrate the impact of IoT security breaches.

1. The Significance of IoT Security:
IoT devices are interconnected, collecting, and exchanging vast amounts of data. Ensuring the security of these devices is crucial to protect user privacy, prevent unauthorized access, and mitigate potential harm caused by compromised devices. Failure to address IoT security risks can result in data breaches, compromised infrastructure, and even physical harm to individuals.

2. Risks and Vulnerabilities in IoT Devices:
- Inadequate Authentication: Many IoT devices come with weak or default passwords, making them vulnerable to brute-force attacks and unauthorized access.
- Lack of Encryption: Insufficient or absent encryption protocols in IoT devices can expose sensitive data during transmission, making it susceptible to interception by attackers.
- Firmware Vulnerabilities: Outdated or unpatched firmware in

IoT devices may contain known vulnerabilities that can be exploited by hackers.
- Lack of Security Updates: IoT devices often lack a mechanism for regular security updates, leaving them exposed to emerging threats.
- Supply Chain Risks: Insecure manufacturing processes or compromised supply chains can introduce vulnerabilities or malicious components into IoT devices.

3. Real-Life Examples of IoT Security Breaches:
- Mirai Botnet: In 2016, the Mirai botnet exploited weak security in IoT devices, such as home routers and IP cameras, to launch large-scale Distributed Denial of Service (DDoS) attacks. This incident highlighted the potential impact of insecure IoT devices when harnessed for malicious purposes.
- Baby Monitor Hacking: There have been cases of attackers gaining unauthorized access to baby monitors, allowing them to observe and even communicate with infants. These incidents demonstrate the vulnerabilities of poorly secured IoT devices and the potential invasion of personal privacy.
- Smart Home Vulnerabilities: Inadequately protected smart home devices, such as smart locks or security cameras, can be compromised, granting unauthorized access to an individual's home and personal information.

4. Best Practices for IoT Security:
- Secure Configuration: Change default passwords, disable unnecessary features, and implement strong authentication mechanisms.
- Encryption: Enable encryption for data transmitted between IoT devices and ensure secure storage of sensitive information.
- Regular Updates: Keep IoT devices up to date with the latest security patches and firmware updates to address known vulnerabilities.
- Network Segmentation: Isolate IoT devices from critical systems through network segmentation to limit the potential impact of a

compromised device.

- User Education: Educate users about the importance of IoT security, including best practices for device setup, password management, and recognizing potential threats.

5. Collaborative Efforts and Standards:

Addressing IoT security requires collaboration among manufacturers, service providers, regulators, and consumers. Industry organizations and standards bodies, such as the Internet Engineering Task Force (IETF) and the Open Web Application Security Project (OWASP), develop guidelines and best practices to promote secure IoT device development and deployment.

In conclusion, IoT security is paramount in safeguarding the privacy and integrity of data, as well as protecting individuals and infrastructure from potential harm. Real-life examples, such as the Mirai botnet and baby monitor hacking incidents, underscore the importance of addressing IoT security vulnerabilities. By implementing secure configurations, regular updates, and user education, we can enhance the overall security of IoT devices and build a more resilient and trustworthy IoT ecosystem. The collaborative efforts of stakeholders across industries and the adherence to established standards will be instrumental in mitigating IoT security risks and ensuring a safer and more secure connected world.

CHAPTER 17: MOBILE DEVICE SECURITY: PROTECTING DATA ON THE GO

Mobile devices have become an integral part of our daily lives, providing us with convenience, connectivity, and access to a wide range of applications and services. However, with this increased reliance on mobile technology comes the need to ensure the security of our devices and the data they contain. This chapter explores the importance of mobile device security, the risks and vulnerabilities associated with mobile devices, and provides real-life examples to illustrate the impact of mobile security breaches.

1. The Significance of Mobile Device Security:
Mobile devices, such as smartphones and tablets, store and transmit vast amounts of personal and sensitive data. Ensuring the security of these devices is crucial to protect user privacy, prevent unauthorized access, and mitigate the risks of data breaches. Failure to address mobile device security can lead to identity theft, financial fraud, and the compromise of personal and corporate data.

2. Risks and Vulnerabilities in Mobile Devices:
- Lost or Stolen Devices: The physical loss or theft of a mobile device can result in unauthorized access to sensitive information stored on the device.

- Malware and Malicious Apps: Mobile devices are susceptible to malware and malicious apps, which can compromise data security, track user activities, or perform unauthorized actions.
- Unsecured Wi-Fi Networks: Connecting to unsecured or malicious Wi-Fi networks can expose mobile devices to data interception, man-in-the-middle attacks, and unauthorized access.
- Phishing Attacks: Mobile devices are targets for phishing attacks, where users may receive fraudulent emails, messages, or links attempting to trick them into providing sensitive information.
- Operating System and App Vulnerabilities: Outdated operating systems or unpatched apps can contain known vulnerabilities that can be exploited by attackers.

3. Real-Life Examples of Mobile Security Breaches:
- Mobile Banking Malware: Malicious apps have been used to target mobile banking users, capturing login credentials and financial information to conduct fraudulent transactions.
- Mobile Ransomware: Ransomware attacks targeting mobile devices have been observed, where attackers encrypt device data and demand a ransom for its release.
- Data Leakage: Incidents have occurred where mobile devices containing sensitive corporate data have been lost or stolen, resulting in the exposure of confidential information.

4. Best Practices for Mobile Device Security:
- Strong Device Authentication: Implement strong passcodes, PINs, or biometric authentication methods to protect device access.
- Regular Updates: Keep mobile device operating systems, apps, and security software up to date to address vulnerabilities and security patches.
- Secure Wi-Fi Connections: Connect to trusted and secure Wi-Fi networks and use Virtual Private Network (VPN) services when accessing public Wi-Fi networks.
- App Security: Only download apps from trusted sources such as

official app stores, review app permissions before installation, and regularly update installed apps.

- Data Encryption and Remote Wiping: Enable device encryption to protect stored data and configure remote wiping capabilities in case of loss or theft.

5. Education and User Awareness:

Promoting mobile security education and user awareness is crucial. Users should be informed about the risks, best practices, and potential security threats associated with mobile devices. Training programs and awareness campaigns can help users make informed decisions and take appropriate security measures to protect their devices and data.

In conclusion, mobile device security is of utmost importance to safeguard personal privacy, corporate data, and financial information. Real-life examples of mobile security breaches, such as mobile banking malware and data leakage incidents, demonstrate the risks associated with inadequate mobile device security. By implementing strong device authentication, regular updates, secure Wi-Fi connections, and user education, we can enhance the overall security posture of mobile devices. Mobile device manufacturers, operating system developers, and app stores also play a vital role in maintaining secure ecosystems. By working together, we can create a safer and more resilient mobile environment that protects user privacy and data in the fast-paced world of mobile technology.

CHAPTER 18: BLOCKCHAIN TECHNOLOGY AND CYBERSECURITY

Blockchain technology has emerged as a transformative force in various industries, revolutionizing the way transactions are conducted and data is stored. Beyond its applications in cryptocurrency, blockchain offers significant potential for enhancing cybersecurity. This chapter explores the fundamentals of blockchain technology, its impact on cybersecurity, and provides real-life examples to illustrate its effectiveness in protecting against cyber threats.

1. Understanding Blockchain Technology:
- Distributed Ledger: Blockchain operates on a decentralized network, where a distributed ledger records and verifies transactions across multiple nodes, ensuring transparency and immutability.
- Cryptographic Security: Blockchain uses cryptographic algorithms to secure data integrity, ensuring that transactions cannot be altered or tampered with.
- Consensus Mechanism: Blockchain employs consensus algorithms, such as Proof of Work or Proof of Stake, to validate transactions and prevent fraudulent activities.

2. Enhancing Cybersecurity with Blockchain Technology:

- Data Integrity and Immutability: The decentralized nature of blockchain makes it difficult for attackers to alter or manipulate data, providing a tamper-proof record of transactions.
- Secure Transactions: Blockchain enables secure peer-to-peer transactions, eliminating the need for intermediaries and reducing the risk of unauthorized access or fraud.
- Identity Management: Blockchain can facilitate secure and decentralized identity management systems, protecting user identities from unauthorized access or identity theft.
- Smart Contracts: Blockchain-based smart contracts can automate and enforce the execution of predefined rules, ensuring secure and reliable transactions without the need for intermediaries.
- Supply Chain Security: Blockchain offers enhanced visibility and traceability in supply chains, reducing the risk of counterfeit products and improving overall supply chain security.

3. Real-Life Examples of Blockchain in Cybersecurity:
- Public Key Infrastructure (PKI): Blockchain can be used to enhance the security of PKI systems by providing a decentralized and tamper-proof ledger for managing digital certificates.
- Decentralized DNS: Blockchain-based decentralized Domain Name Systems (DNS) can prevent DNS hijacking and improve the security and resilience of internet infrastructure.
- Data Protection: Blockchain can enable secure and transparent data sharing, ensuring data integrity and protecting against unauthorized access or data breaches.
- IoT Security: Blockchain can enhance the security of Internet of Things (IoT) devices by enabling secure device authentication, data integrity, and decentralized control.

4. Challenges and Considerations:
While blockchain technology offers significant cybersecurity benefits, it also presents challenges and considerations:
- Scalability: Blockchain networks currently face scalability limitations, making it challenging to handle a high volume of

transactions in real-time.

- Governance and Regulation: The decentralized nature of blockchain raises questions around governance, legal frameworks, and regulatory compliance.

- Key Management: Proper key management is crucial to ensure the security of blockchain-based systems, as the loss or compromise of private keys can lead to unauthorized access or loss of data.

5. The Future of Blockchain and Cybersecurity:

Blockchain technology continues to evolve, with ongoing research and development focused on addressing its limitations and expanding its applications in cybersecurity. Collaborative efforts between industry, academia, and government are crucial to unlock the full potential of blockchain in securing digital systems and protecting against cyber threats.

In conclusion, blockchain technology has the potential to revolutionize cybersecurity by providing enhanced data integrity, secure transactions, and decentralized identity management. Real-life examples, such as blockchain's application in PKI, decentralized DNS, and data protection, demonstrate its effectiveness in addressing cybersecurity challenges. While challenges exist, ongoing advancements in blockchain technology and collaborative efforts will pave the way for a more secure and resilient digital future. Organizations and individuals should explore the potential of blockchain in their cybersecurity strategies to mitigate risks and protect against evolving cyber threats.

CHAPTER 19:
BIOMETRICS
AND IDENTITY
MANAGEMENT

In an increasingly digital world, the need for secure and reliable identity verification is paramount. Biometrics, a field that utilizes unique physical and behavioural characteristics for identification, has emerged as a powerful solution. This chapter explores the role of biometrics in identity management, its applications, benefits, challenges, and real-life examples of its implementation.

1. Understanding Biometrics:
Biometrics is the measurement and analysis of unique physical or behavioural characteristics for identification or authentication purposes. It includes various modalities such as fingerprints, iris scans, facial recognition, voice recognition, and behavioural biometrics like keystroke dynamics or gait analysis. Biometric systems capture these characteristics, convert them into digital representations, and match them against stored templates for identity verification.

2. Applications of Biometrics in Identity Management:
- Border Control: Biometric systems are extensively used in border control processes for accurate and efficient verification of travellers, enhancing security and preventing identity fraud.
- Law Enforcement: Biometrics aid law enforcement agencies in

identifying criminals through fingerprint or facial recognition systems, helping solve crimes and maintain public safety.
- Access Control: Biometric authentication is employed to secure physical and digital access to facilities, devices, or information, reducing the reliance on traditional methods like passwords or access cards.
- Financial Services: Biometrics play a vital role in enhancing security and convenience in financial transactions, with fingerprint or facial recognition used for mobile banking or payment applications.
- Healthcare: Biometrics ensure accurate patient identification, reducing medical errors and fraud in healthcare systems, and enabling secure access to electronic health records.

3. Benefits of Biometrics in Identity Management:
- Enhanced Security: Biometrics offer a higher level of security than traditional methods since they are based on unique physiological or behavioural traits that are difficult to forge or replicate.
- Convenience and User Experience: Biometrics eliminate the need for remembering and managing multiple passwords or carrying access cards, providing a seamless and user-friendly authentication experience.
- Accuracy and Efficiency: Biometric systems provide fast and accurate identification, reducing the chances of false positives or negatives and streamlining identity verification processes.
- Fraud Prevention: Biometrics significantly mitigate identity fraud by ensuring that individuals can be reliably linked to their unique biometric characteristics, minimizing the risk of impersonation.

4. Challenges and Considerations:
- Privacy Concerns: The collection and storage of biometric data raise privacy concerns regarding data protection, consent, and potential misuse. Robust security measures and adherence to privacy regulations are essential.

- Error Rates and False Matches: Biometric systems may encounter errors due to factors like environmental conditions, aging, or changes in an individual's biometric traits. False matches can occur, necessitating appropriate algorithms and quality control mechanisms.
- Ethical Considerations: The use of biometrics raises ethical questions regarding consent, surveillance, and potential biases. Fairness, transparency, and accountability should be prioritized in the deployment and use of biometric systems.

5. Real-Life Examples of Biometrics in Identity Management:
- Aadhaar System: India's Aadhaar, the world's largest biometric identification program, has enrolled over a billion people using iris and fingerprint scans, facilitating secure access to government services.
- Mobile Biometrics: Mobile devices increasingly integrate fingerprint or facial recognition as a convenient and secure authentication method, enhancing user access control and mobile payments.
- Airport Biometric Systems: Airports worldwide have implemented biometric solutions, such as facial recognition, to expedite passenger processing, improve security, and enhance the travel experience.

In conclusion, biometrics plays a pivotal role in identity management, offering enhanced security, convenience, and accuracy. Real-life examples like the Aadhaar system and airport biometric deployments showcase its effectiveness in various domains. However, privacy concerns, error rates, and ethical considerations must be addressed to ensure responsible and trustworthy implementation. As biometric technology advances, organizations and governments must strike a balance between security, privacy, and usability to build robust and inclusive identity management systems for the digital age.

PART V: ADDRESSING CYBERSECURITY CHALLENGES

CHAPTER 20: CYBERSECURITY REGULATIONS AND COMPLIANCE

In today's interconnected and data-driven world, cybersecurity regulations and compliance frameworks play a crucial role in safeguarding sensitive information, protecting individuals' privacy, and maintaining the integrity of digital systems. This chapter explores the importance of cybersecurity regulations, compliance requirements, their impact on organizations, and real-life examples of regulatory frameworks in practice.

1. Understanding Cybersecurity Regulations:
Cybersecurity regulations are legal frameworks designed to establish guidelines, standards, and requirements for organizations to protect their information systems and the data they handle. These regulations aim to mitigate cyber risks, promote good security practices, and ensure the confidentiality, integrity, and availability of information.

2. Importance of Cybersecurity Regulations:
- Protection of Sensitive Data: Regulations help safeguard personal and sensitive information, including financial data, medical records, and personally identifiable information (PII), from unauthorized access, disclosure, or misuse.
- Mitigation of Cyber Risks: Regulations require organizations

to implement security controls and risk management processes to identify, assess, and mitigate cyber threats, reducing the likelihood and impact of cyberattacks.

- Preserving Trust and Confidence: Compliance with regulations enhances customer trust and confidence, as individuals feel reassured that their information is being handled securely and that organizations are taking proactive measures to protect their data.

- Harmonization and Consistency: Regulations provide a unified approach to cybersecurity, ensuring that organizations across industries and jurisdictions follow similar standards and best practices.

3. Key Cybersecurity Regulations and Compliance Frameworks:

- General Data Protection Regulation (GDPR): Implemented in the European Union, the GDPR focuses on protecting the privacy and personal data of EU citizens and imposes strict requirements on data controllers and processors.

- California Consumer Privacy Act (CCPA): Enacted in California, this regulation enhances consumer privacy rights and imposes obligations on businesses regarding the collection, use, and disclosure of personal information.

- Payment Card Industry Data Security Standard (PCI DSS): Developed by major credit card companies, PCI DSS establishes security requirements for organizations that handle payment card data, aiming to prevent payment card fraud.

- Health Insurance Portability and Accountability Act (HIPAA): HIPAA sets standards for protecting individuals' health information, ensuring its confidentiality, integrity, and availability in the healthcare industry.

- ISO/IEC 27001: This international standard provides a framework for implementing an information security management system (ISMS), encompassing policies, procedures, and controls to manage information security risks effectively.

4. Impact of Cybersecurity Regulations on Organizations:

- Increased Accountability: Regulations hold organizations accountable for protecting data and maintaining robust security measures, necessitating the development of comprehensive security programs.
- Compliance Costs: Organizations may incur expenses related to implementing security controls, conducting audits, and ensuring ongoing compliance with regulatory requirements.
- Reputational Impact: Failure to comply with regulations can damage an organization's reputation and result in legal consequences, loss of customer trust, and financial penalties.
- Competitive Advantage: Demonstrating compliance with cybersecurity regulations can provide a competitive edge by instilling confidence in customers, partners, and stakeholders.

5. Real-Life Examples of Cybersecurity Regulations in Practice:
- European Union's GDPR: The GDPR has led to significant changes in how organizations handle personal data, requiring them to obtain explicit consent, implement privacy by design principles, and report data breaches within strict timelines.
- New York Department of Financial Services (NYDFS) Cybersecurity Regulation: This regulation applies to financial institutions in New York State and mandates specific cybersecurity measures, including the adoption of robust risk assessment programs and multi-factor authentication.
- NIST Cybersecurity Framework: Developed by the National Institute of Standards and Technology (NIST) in the United States, this voluntary framework provides a set of best practices, standards, and guidelines for organizations to manage and improve their cybersecurity posture.

In conclusion, cybersecurity regulations and compliance frameworks are instrumental in mitigating cyber risks, protecting sensitive information, and maintaining trust in the digital ecosystem. Real-life examples like the GDPR, NYDFS Cybersecurity Regulation, and the NIST Cybersecurity Framework demonstrate the impact and practical application of regulatory frameworks.

Organizations must stay abreast of evolving regulations, develop robust security programs, and ensure ongoing compliance to effectively navigate the complex cybersecurity landscape and protect their digital assets and stakeholders' interests.

CHAPTER 21: CYBERSECURITY FOR SMALL AND MEDIUM-SIZED ENTERPRISES (SMES)

In today's digital landscape, small and medium-sized enterprises (SMEs) face increasing cybersecurity threats that can have severe consequences on their operations, finances, and reputation. This chapter explores the unique cybersecurity challenges faced by SMEs, provides practical guidance for strengthening their security posture, and discusses real-life examples of cybersecurity incidents and best practices.

1. Understanding the Cybersecurity Landscape for SMEs:
- Growing Target: SMEs are increasingly targeted by cybercriminals due to their perceived vulnerabilities, limited resources for cybersecurity, and valuable customer data they possess.
- Impact of Cyberattacks: A cybersecurity incident can lead to financial losses, business disruption, reputational damage, loss of customer trust, and potential legal and regulatory consequences.
- Unique Challenges: SMEs often lack dedicated IT and cybersecurity staff, have limited budgets for cybersecurity investments, and may have less awareness of cyber threats and

best practices compared to larger enterprises.

2. Key Cybersecurity Threats for SMEs:
- Phishing Attacks: Cybercriminals use deceptive emails and messages to trick employees into revealing sensitive information or downloading malicious software.
- Ransomware: SMEs are frequently targeted with ransomware attacks that encrypt their data, demanding a ransom for its release.
- Business Email Compromise (BEC): Attackers impersonate executives or trusted contacts to trick SMEs into making fraudulent payments or disclosing sensitive information.
- Insider Threats: Disgruntled employees or individuals with access to sensitive data can intentionally cause harm to the organization.
- Third-Party Risks: SMEs often rely on third-party vendors or service providers, increasing the potential for supply chain attacks and data breaches.

3. Strengthening Cybersecurity in SMEs:
- Risk Assessment: SMEs should conduct a comprehensive risk assessment to identify their critical assets, potential vulnerabilities, and threats they face.
- Employee Education and Awareness: Training employees on cybersecurity best practices, including password hygiene, recognizing phishing attempts, and reporting suspicious activities, is crucial.
- Secure Network Infrastructure: Implementing firewalls, secure Wi-Fi networks, and strong access controls helps protect SMEs from unauthorized access.
- Regular Software Updates and Patching: Keeping operating systems, applications, and security software up to date helps address known vulnerabilities.
- Data Backup and Recovery: Regularly backing up important data and having a reliable recovery plan in place can mitigate the impact of ransomware attacks and data loss.

- Incident Response Plan: SMEs should develop an incident response plan that outlines the steps to be taken in case of a cybersecurity incident, including reporting and communication procedures.

4. Real-Life Examples and Best Practices:
- Example 1: The "WannaCry" Ransomware Attack in 2017 affected numerous organizations worldwide, including SMEs. It highlighted the importance of regular software updates and patching to protect against known vulnerabilities.
- Example 2: A small online retailer experienced a data breach due to a third-party vendor's compromised system. This incident underscores the need for SMEs to assess the security practices of their vendors and maintain strong vendor management procedures.
- Best Practice 1: Implementing multi-factor authentication (MFA) adds an extra layer of security to protect against unauthorized access to systems and accounts.
- Best Practice 2: SMEs can leverage cloud-based security services, such as managed security service providers (MSSPs), to enhance their security capabilities without requiring extensive in-house expertise.

In conclusion, SMEs are increasingly targeted by cyber threats, necessitating a proactive approach to cybersecurity. By understanding the unique challenges, they face, implementing best practices, and learning from real-life examples, SMEs can enhance their cybersecurity posture and better protect their operations and sensitive data. Ultimately, prioritizing cybersecurity safeguards SMEs from financial losses, reputational damage, and potential legal consequences, enabling them to thrive in an increasingly digital business environment.

CHAPTER 22:
CYBERSECURITY
IN CRITICAL
INFRASTRUCTURE

In today's interconnected world, critical infrastructure systems play a vital role in supporting essential services and maintaining the functioning of societies. However, with increased digitization and connectivity, these systems have become prime targets for cyber threats. This chapter explores the significance of cybersecurity in critical infrastructure, the potential consequences of cyberattacks, and real-life examples of cyber incidents in various sectors.

1. Understanding Critical Infrastructure:
- Definition: Critical infrastructure encompasses sectors such as energy, transportation, healthcare, telecommunications, water and wastewater, and financial services that are essential for the functioning of society.
- Interdependencies: Critical infrastructure systems are interconnected, with disruptions in one sector potentially impacting others and causing cascading effects.
- Importance of Security: The reliable and secure operation of critical infrastructure is crucial for public safety, national security, and economic stability.

2. Cybersecurity Challenges in Critical Infrastructure:
- Unique Characteristics: Critical infrastructure systems often have legacy technologies, complex networks, and extended lifecycles, making them susceptible to vulnerabilities.
- Cyber Threat Landscape: Nation-states, hacktivists, criminal organizations, and even insider threats pose significant risks to critical infrastructure.
- Potential Consequences: Cyberattacks on critical infrastructure can result in disruptions to essential services, financial losses, environmental damage, and even loss of life.

3. Real-Life Examples of Cyber Incidents in Critical Infrastructure:
- Example 1: Stuxnet Worm (2010): This sophisticated malware specifically targeted industrial control systems (ICS) used in nuclear facilities, causing physical damage to centrifuges and highlighting the potential impact of cyberattacks on critical infrastructure.
- Example 2: Ukraine Power Grid Attack (2015 and 2016): Hackers disrupted the power grid in Ukraine, causing widespread power outages, affecting thousands of people. This incident emphasized the vulnerability of critical infrastructure systems to cyber threats.
- Example 3: WannaCry Ransomware Attack (2017): Although not specifically targeting critical infrastructure, the WannaCry attack affected numerous organizations globally, including healthcare systems, demonstrating the potential for cyber incidents to disrupt critical services.

4. Enhancing Cybersecurity in Critical Infrastructure:
- Risk Assessment and Management: Conducting thorough risk assessments and implementing risk management strategies tailored to critical infrastructure systems are essential.
- Robust Access Controls: Implementing strong access controls, including multi-factor authentication, helps protect critical systems from unauthorized access.
- Continuous Monitoring and Threat Intelligence: Deploying

robust monitoring systems and leveraging threat intelligence enables early detection and response to potential cyber threats.

- Incident Response and Recovery: Having well-defined incident response plans and procedures helps minimize the impact of cyber incidents and ensures timely recovery.

- Collaboration and Information Sharing: Building partnerships between government agencies, private sector organizations, and industry associations fosters collaboration and enables the exchange of information and best practices.

In conclusion, cybersecurity in critical infrastructure is of utmost importance to safeguard essential services and ensure public safety. The interconnected nature of critical infrastructure systems, coupled with the evolving cyber threat landscape, requires a comprehensive and proactive approach to cybersecurity. By learning from real-life examples, implementing robust security measures, and fostering collaboration between stakeholders, critical infrastructure can be better protected against cyber threats. Enhancing cybersecurity in critical infrastructure not only mitigates the potential consequences of cyberattacks but also contributes to the resilience and stability of nations and societies as they rely on these critical services to thrive.

CHAPTER 23: INTERNATIONAL COOPERATION IN CYBERSECURITY

In today's interconnected and digitized world, cyber threats transcend national boundaries, making international cooperation crucial in addressing the global challenges of cybersecurity. This chapter explores the importance of international collaboration in cybersecurity, key organizations and initiatives promoting cooperation, and real-life examples of successful international cybersecurity cooperation efforts.

1. The Need for International Cooperation in Cybersecurity:
- Global Nature of Cyber Threats: Cyberattacks can originate from anywhere and target entities across borders, posing a significant challenge to individual nations' cybersecurity efforts.
- Shared Responsibility: Cybersecurity is a shared responsibility that requires collective action to combat cybercrime, promote information sharing, and strengthen defences.
- Harmonizing Standards and Practices: International cooperation helps in establishing common cybersecurity standards, best practices, and norms, facilitating the development of a cohesive global cybersecurity framework.

2. Key Organizations and Initiatives:

- United Nations (UN): The UN promotes international cooperation in cybersecurity through various initiatives, including the UN Group of Governmental Experts (GGE) on Developments in the Field of Information and Telecommunications in the Context of International Security.
- International Telecommunication Union (ITU): As a specialized agency of the UN, the ITU works to enhance cybersecurity capabilities globally and facilitates collaboration among member states.
- NATO Cooperative Cyber Defence Centre of Excellence (CCDCOE): The CCDCOE is a multinational organization that conducts research, training, and exercises to enhance cybersecurity and foster international cooperation.
- Five Eyes and Other Information Sharing Alliances: Intelligence alliances, such as the Five Eyes (Australia, Canada, New Zealand, the United Kingdom, and the United States), facilitate information sharing on cyber threats and intelligence to enhance cybersecurity efforts.

3. Real-Life Examples of International Cybersecurity Cooperation:
- Budapest Convention on Cybercrime: The Budapest Convention is the first international treaty addressing cybercrime. It promotes cooperation among signatory countries in combating cyber threats, exchanging information, and facilitating cross-border investigations.
- Interpol's Global Complex for Innovation (IGCI): The IGCI serves as a centre for fostering international collaboration in cybercrime investigations, providing operational support, and facilitating information sharing among member countries.
- European Union Agency for Cybersecurity (ENISA): ENISA promotes cooperation and provides expertise on cybersecurity matters to EU member states, facilitating the exchange of best practices and promoting cybersecurity resilience across Europe.
- International Cybersecurity Dialogue: Bilateral and multilateral cybersecurity dialogues between countries aim to foster trust, enhance cooperation, and address common cybersecurity

challenges.

4. Benefits and Challenges of International Cooperation:
- Benefits: International cooperation in cybersecurity allows for the pooling of resources, expertise, and intelligence, enabling faster response to cyber threats and improved resilience. It promotes the sharing of best practices, capacity-building, and the development of coordinated cybersecurity strategies.
- Challenges: National interests, legal frameworks, and differing priorities can present challenges to effective international cooperation. Information sharing may be hindered by concerns over sovereignty, privacy, and the protection of classified information.

In conclusion, international cooperation is essential to effectively address the global nature of cyber threats. By promoting information sharing, capacity-building, and the harmonization of cybersecurity standards, countries can collectively strengthen their defences against cyberattacks. Real-life examples, such as the Budapest Convention, Interpol's IGCI, and regional cybersecurity organizations, demonstrate the success and importance of international cooperation in combating cybercrime. As cyber threats continue to evolve, sustained international collaboration is vital to creating a secure and resilient digital environment for individuals, organizations, and nations worldwide.

CHAPTER 24:
THE FUTURE OF
CYBERSECURITY:
ANTICIPATING
AND MITIGATING
FUTURE THREATS

As technology continues to advance rapidly, the cybersecurity landscape faces new and evolving threats. This chapter explores the future of cybersecurity, including emerging trends, potential challenges, and strategies for anticipating and mitigating future threats. Real-life examples of innovative solutions and initiatives will be discussed to illustrate the importance of proactive cybersecurity measures.

1. The Changing Cybersecurity Landscape:
- Evolving Threat Landscape: Cybercriminals are becoming increasingly sophisticated, using advanced techniques such as artificial intelligence and machine learning to launch complex and targeted attacks.
- Internet of Things (IoT): The proliferation of interconnected devices in the IoT poses significant cybersecurity challenges, as vulnerabilities in IoT devices can be exploited to gain

unauthorized access or launch attacks.

- Cloud Computing: The widespread adoption of cloud computing introduces new security considerations, including data breaches, unauthorized access, and cloud service provider vulnerabilities.

2. Emerging Trends and Technologies:

- Artificial Intelligence (AI) and Machine Learning (ML): AI and ML can be used to enhance cybersecurity defences by automating threat detection, analysing vast amounts of data for anomalies, and predicting and preventing cyber-attacks.

- Quantum Computing: The advent of quantum computing threatens current encryption algorithms, highlighting the need for post-quantum cryptographic solutions to secure sensitive information.

- Biometric Authentication: Biometric authentication, such as fingerprint or facial recognition, is gaining popularity as a more secure alternative to traditional password-based authentication methods.

3. Challenges in Future Cybersecurity:

- Insider Threats: Insider threats, where trusted individuals misuse their privileges or share sensitive information, remain a significant challenge for organizations and require robust access controls and monitoring mechanisms.

- Supply Chain Attacks: Cybercriminals may target the supply chain to gain unauthorized access to systems or introduce malicious components, emphasizing the importance of vetting and securing third-party vendors.

- Cybersecurity Skills Gap: The demand for cybersecurity professionals exceeds the supply, creating a skills gap that needs to be addressed through education, training, and fostering a cybersecurity workforce.

4. Strategies for Anticipating and Mitigating Future Threats:

- Threat Intelligence and Information Sharing: Sharing threat intelligence among organizations and collaborating with industry peers and government entities can help identify and respond to emerging threats more effectively.

- Proactive Vulnerability Management: Regular vulnerability assessments, penetration testing, and patch management are crucial to identifying and remedying security weaknesses before they can be exploited.

- Security by Design: Incorporating security principles from the initial stages of system development, such as secure coding practices and robust architecture design, can enhance the overall security posture.

- Continuous Monitoring and Incident Response: Implementing a comprehensive monitoring system and establishing an incident response plan can help detect and respond to cyber threats in real-time, minimizing the impact of security incidents.

Real-Life Examples:

- Stuxnet: The Stuxnet worm, discovered in 2010, targeted Iran's nuclear facilities and is considered one of the most sophisticated cyber-attacks in history. It highlighted the potential damage that can be caused by nation-state-sponsored attacks and the need for strong defences against advanced threats.

- Bug Bounty Programs: Many organizations, including tech giants like Google and Microsoft, have implemented bug bounty programs that reward individuals for discovering and reporting vulnerabilities. These programs harness the power of the global cybersecurity community to identify and address vulnerabilities before they can be exploited.

- Zero Trust Architecture: Zero Trust is an approach to cybersecurity that assumes no trust by default and requires strict authentication and authorization measures for every user and device accessing the network. It emphasizes the principle of "never trust, always verify" and has gained traction in recent years as a way to enhance security.

In conclusion, the future of cybersecurity holds both challenges and opportunities. As new technologies emerge, it is essential to anticipate and mitigate future threats proactively. By embracing emerging trends, fostering collaboration and information sharing, and adopting a proactive and security-centric approach, organizations and individuals can stay ahead of cyber threats and create a secure digital environment. Real-life examples, such as the Stuxnet attack, bug bounty programs, and the implementation of Zero Trust architecture, demonstrate the importance of staying vigilant and adaptive in the face of evolving cyber threats. By adopting these strategies and learning from past incidents, we can build a resilient cybersecurity landscape to protect our digital infrastructure and safeguard sensitive information in the future.

www.ingramcontent.com/pod-product-compliance
Lightning Source LLC
LaVergne TN
LVHW051537050326
832903LV00033B/4288